Why Did Jesus Weep?

Joshua Rhoades

Published by Joshua Paul Rhoades, 2024.

WHY DID JESUS WEEP?

First edition. September 23, 2024.

Copyright © 2024 Joshua Rhoades.

ISBN: 979-8227433152

Written by Joshua Rhoades.

Also by Joshua Rhoades

Courage Under Fire: David's Stand On The Battlefield
Jonah's Journey: Voices Of Redemption And Lessons In Obedience
The Furnace Of Faith: 12 Principles From The Heat Of Faith
Whispers of Hope: Inspiring Stories of Men's Prayers In Scripture
Frontier Legends: The Oregon Dream
Elijah: A Beacon Of Boldness
HOOK, LINE & SAVIOUR - Faith Reflections from Fishing
Driven By Faith: Motor Racing Inspired Christian Life
30 Day Devotional - Bold and Strong- Coffee Devotions for a Courageous Christian Walk
Authentic Christianity: The Heart of Old Time Religion
Consider The Ant - God's Tiny Preachers
Flee Fornication: The Plea For Purity
Renewed Hope- How to Find Encouragement in God
Sounding The Call - The Voice of Conviction
The Altar - Where Heaven Meets Earth
The Bible's Battlefields- Timeless Lessons from Ancient Wars
The Sacred Art of Silence - How Silence Speaks in Scripture
Under Fire- The Sanctity of the Traditional Biblical Home
Who Is on the Lord's Side? A Call to Righteousness
What Is Truth? - From Skepticism to Submission
First and Goal- Faith and Football Fundamentals
From Dugout to Devotion- Spiritual Lessons from Baseball
Par for the Course- Faith and Fairways
The Believer's Pace- Tools for Running Life's Marathon
The Immutable Fortress- Security in God's Unchanging Nature
Biblical Bravery
Deer Stands and Devotions: A Hunter's Walk with God

Jesus Knows- Our Hearts, Our Responsibility
Restoration - Setting The Bone
Spiritual 911- God's Word for Life's Emergency's
The Freedom of Forgiveness
The Jezebel Effect - Ancient Manipulations Modern Lessons
The Shout That Stopped The Saviour
The Time Machine Chronicles: Old Testament Characters
Anchored In Truth Exploring The Depths of Psalm 119
Biblical Counsel on Anger
Proverbs' Portraits The Men God Mentions
Stumbling in the Dark - The Dangers of Alcohol
Guarding the Wicket Protecting Your Faith and Game
The Champion's Faith - Wrestling and Achieving Spiritual Victory
Scriptural Commands for Modern Times Living God's Word Today Volume 1
Scriptural Commands for Modern Times Living God's Word Today Volume 2
Scriptural Commands for Modern Times Living God's Word TodayVolume3
The Greatest Gift
A Christmas Journey of Faith
Daughter Of The King: Embracing Your Identity In Christ
Determination and Dedication Building Strong Faith As A Young Man
Walking Through Walls God's Power to Part the Storms of Life
David's Song Of Deliverance Praising God Through Every Storm
From Weakness to Warrior: Gideon's Transformation
Why Did Jesus Weep?

Dedication

To you, the reader, who has opened this book seeking answers, I dedicate these words to the heart behind your search. You may be walking through the valley of grief, weighed down by loss, sorrow, or the relentless storms of life. Maybe you've experienced moments where you've asked, Where is God in my pain? Perhaps you've wondered why the tears keep flowing, or why you can't seem to find the light in the darkness. To you—whether you are weary, heartbroken, or simply seeking to understand the depths of Christ's compassion—I offer this book as a reminder that you are not alone.

This book, "Why Did Jesus Weep?", is written for those who long to know the Savior who wept. It's written for those who have cried until there seemed to be no more tears left, for those who feel the crushing weight of a broken world. It's for the parents grieving a child, the spouse grieving a partner, the friend grieving the loss of companionship, and for anyone who has ever felt the bitter sting of loss, isolation, or despair.

But it is also written for those who have come to the other side of their grief, holding onto hope with trembling hands, still wondering why God allowed such pain. It's for the ones who now want to understand what those tears meant—both theirs and Christ's.

In Jesus' weeping at the tomb of Lazarus, we see not just a glimpse of His humanity, but a revelation of His heart. When Jesus wept, He entered fully into the human experience of sorrow. He didn't stand apart, unaffected by the pain of those around Him. Instead, He wept alongside them, showing us that our tears are seen, understood, and shared by the very God who created us.

To you, the reader, this book is a love letter from the heart of a Savior who weeps with you. It is a message of comfort that declares, "You are not alone in your sorrow." Jesus knows your pain—intimately. And not only does He weep with you, but He also has the power to redeem that very pain. He stands at the threshold of your despair, ready to turn mourning into dancing, ashes into beauty, tears into hope.

As you read these pages, my prayer is that you will find solace in the knowledge that Jesus doesn't just stand on the sidelines of your suffering. He steps into it with you, wraps you in His grace, and whispers that He is with you—every step, every tear, every heartache. His weeping is not a moment of weakness but a promise that He is close to the brokenhearted and saves those who are crushed in spirit.

I dedicate this book to your healing, your hope, and your journey with the One who wept, not just to comfort, but to conquer. Through His tears, may you find the courage to believe that He is working all things for good, even when the night is long, and the morning feels far away. May you rest in the assurance that the same Savior who wept also rose, triumphant, offering you new life and unshakable hope. His tears are not the end of the story, but the beginning of something beautiful—a story of redemption, renewal, and resurrection.

May you find peace in His weeping and strength in His love. You are held by the One who weeps and the One who overcomes.

With compassion and hope,

Joshua Rhoades

Introduction

In the story of Lazarus in John 11, we encounter one of the most profound and emotional moments in Jesus' earthly ministry: His weeping. This simple yet powerful act raises an important question—Why Did Jesus Weep? Was it merely a reaction to the grief around Him, or was there something deeper behind His tears? This book explores lessons that reveal the depth of Jesus' compassion and His divine response to human suffering. Through these lessons, we discover that Jesus' tears were not just a fleeting response to Lazarus' death but a profound expression of His empathy, love, and understanding of the world's brokenness.

Jesus' tears at the tomb of Lazarus hold a timeless significance. They show us that He is not a distant Savior but intimately involved in our lives, sharing our pain and grief. His tears reflect His investment in the suffering of humanity, demonstrating that He feels the weight of our burdens and enters into our struggles with us. Each lesson in this book—from Death's Devastation to the Desire for Restoration—reveals a different facet of why Jesus wept and how His tears reflect His heart for us. Jesus' weeping was not just for those present at the tomb but for all of us who experience the pain of loss, the weight of doubt, and the devastation of a broken world.

Moreover, Jesus' tears were not a sign of weakness but a testimony to His divine purpose. Following His weeping, Jesus performed one of His greatest miracles—raising Lazarus from the dead. This act foreshadowed His resurrection and His ultimate triumph over sin and death. His tears remind us that Jesus' love and compassion are deeply intertwined with His power and authority. His weeping was not just an emotional response but a declaration of His commitment to bring life out of death, hope out of despair, and restoration to a broken world. Through these lessons, we are invited to trust in Jesus not only as the one who feels our pain but as the one who has the power to transform it.

For Christians today, the question is, Why Did Jesus Weep? offers a compelling challenge: How do we continue in our walk with Christ, trusting in His power, love, and promises, even in the face of suffering? Jesus' tears invite us to reflect on how we respond to our pain and the pain of those around us. Do we trust that He is with us in our darkest moments? Are we willing to follow His example of compassion, sharing in the burdens of others and offering them the hope that He provides?

This book reminds us that Jesus' tears were not just for a single moment in time but a message for all of us. He weeps with us, understands our pain, and desires to bring healing and hope to a broken world. As we journey through these lessons, may we find comfort in the knowledge that Jesus' love is deep, authentic, and enduring and that His victory over death offers us the ultimate hope of new life in Him.

Chapter 1 - Death's Devastation

In John 11, we witness one of the most poignant moments in Scripture where Jesus, the Son of God, weeps at the death of His friend Lazarus. This simple yet powerful display of emotion highlights the depth of Jesus' compassion and His identification with the human experience. The reason for Jesus' tears lies in Death's Devastation, a devastating reality that profoundly affects everyone and was never part of God's original plan for humanity. When we read John 11:33, "When Jesus therefore saw her weeping, and the Jews also weeping which came with her, he groaned in the spirit, and was troubled," we are given insight into the profound grief that overwhelmed the people surrounding Lazarus' tomb. The text tells us that Jesus was deeply moved and troubled in His spirit when He saw the grief of Mary, Martha, and the Jews who had come to mourn Lazarus. Their collective sorrow stirred Jesus emotionally, leading Him to weep. This moment reveals several important lessons about Jesus' response to death and how it reflects His humanity and His divine mission.

First, Jesus' tears show His deep empathy and compassion for mournful people. Death is an undeniable part of the human experience, and it brings with it a unique pain and sorrow that words often cannot fully express. Jesus, fully human and fully divine, entered into the human condition by experiencing the grief that death brings. His tears demonstrate that He is not a distant or aloof Savior but One who profoundly cares about our sorrows. Even though He knew that He was about to raise Lazarus from the dead, Jesus wept because He was moved by the sadness of those He loved. This highlights that God is not indifferent to our pain; He is intimately aware and deeply moved by it.

Furthermore, Jesus' tears reveal the brokenness of the world caused by sin. Initially, God created the world without death, pain, or suffering. Humanity was meant to live in perfect harmony with God, free from the devastation of death. However, when sin entered the world through Adam and Eve's disobedience, death became a tragic part of the human experience. Romans 5:12 says, "Wherefore, as by one man sin entered into the world, and death by sin; and so death passed upon all men, for that all have sinned." Jesus wept because He saw firsthand the consequences of sin, which included death and the resulting heartache it brings. His tears reflect His deep sorrow over the brokenness of the world and the separation that death causes between loved ones. Even though Jesus had come to defeat death once and for all, He still grieved over the impact it had on those He cared about.

Another key aspect of Jesus' weeping reflects His connection to Lazarus and His genuine love for him. The Bible clarifies that Jesus had a close relationship with Lazarus and his sisters, Mary and Martha. John 11:35, the shortest verse in the Bible, simply states, "Jesus wept." This verse, though brief, carries immense weight. It shows us that Jesus was not immune to personal grief. He was deeply affected by the death of His friend. The Jews who were present even remarked, "Behold how he loved him!" (John 11:36). Jesus' weeping was not just a display of compassion for the crowd but also a reflection of His sorrow at losing a dear friend. This emphasizes that Jesus, despite His divine power and knowledge, felt the emotional weight of human loss just as we do.

Jesus' tears also speak to the broader impact of death on all humanity. As the Son of God, Jesus was not just grieving for Lazarus alone but for the entirety of humanity and the suffering caused by death throughout the ages. Death, from a biblical perspective, is the ultimate enemy of humanity. It represents separation—not just from loved ones but also from God. Jesus wept because death is a painful reminder of the fall of humanity and the broken relationship between God and man. In this sense, Jesus' tears can be seen as an expression of His sorrow for the world as a whole, a world that has been ravaged by sin and death. His weeping reminds us that death was never part of God's original design, and Jesus came to restore what was lost through His death and resurrection.

However, Jesus' weeping does not indicate hopelessness. On the contrary, it sets the stage for the incredible miracle that follows—the raising of Lazarus from the dead. Jesus' tears are a prelude to the victory He will demonstrate over death. While He fully enters into the grief of the moment, He also knows that death will not have the final word. In John 11:25-26, Jesus says to Martha, "I am the resurrection, and the life: he that believeth in me, though he were dead, yet shall he live: And whosoever liveth and believeth in me shall never die." Jesus clarifies that He has the power to conquer death and that eternal life is available to all who believe in Him. His weeping is not a sign of defeat but a testament to His deep care for those who mourn and His desire to offer hope in the face of death.

In this moment, Jesus' weeping challenges us to reflect on our responses to the suffering and pain we see around us. Just as Jesus was moved to compassion by the grief of others, we too are called to weep with those who weep and mourn with those who mourn (Romans 12:15). Jesus' tears show us that it is not enough to remain detached from the suffering of others. Instead, we are called to enter into their pain, just as Jesus entered into the grief of Mary and Martha. His example teaches us the importance of empathy and the power of shared sorrow. In a world where death and suffering are inevitable, our compassion and love for others can serve as a reflection of Christ's heart.

Furthermore, Jesus' weeping can also be seen as a call to action for believers. While we grieve the effects of death, we are also called to offer hope to those who are suffering. Jesus did not just weep at Lazarus' tomb; He also raised Lazarus from the dead. In the same way, we are called to offer hope and comfort to grieving people by pointing them to the truth of the gospel. Jesus' victory over death through His resurrection provides the ultimate hope for all who believe in Him. Christians are responsible for sharing this hope with others, reminding them that death is not the end for those who trust in Christ.

Finally, Jesus' weeping at the tomb of Lazarus points to the ultimate purpose of His coming—to defeat death once and for all. His tears were not just for the moment, but for the greater reality He came to address. Jesus knew that in a short time, He would face His death on the cross, which would pave the way for the salvation of humanity. His weeping foreshadows the sorrow He would experience on the cross as He bore the weight of the world's sin and death. Yet, through His sacrifice, Jesus would conquer death and offer eternal life to all who believe. His tears remind us of the depth of His love and the lengths He would go to bring life out of death.

In conclusion, Jesus' weeping in John 11 is a powerful demonstration of His compassion, empathy, and love for humanity. Death's Devastation moved Him to tears because He saw the profound grief and sorrow it brought to those He loved. His tears reflect His identification with our pain, His sorrow over the world's brokenness, and His desire to bring restoration and hope. Yet, His weeping was not a sign of defeat but a prelude to the victory He would achieve over death. Through His resurrection of Lazarus, and ultimately through His resurrection, Jesus shows He has the power to defeat death and offer eternal life. His tears, then, are a reminder that while death brings sorrow, it does not have the final word. In Christ, we have the hope of eternal life, and we are called to share this hope with others, offering comfort and compassion to grieving people. Jesus' weeping at Lazarus' tomb is a testament to His deep love for humanity and His desire to bring life out of death. Through His tears, we see the heart of a Savior who is with us in our pain and offers us the hope of resurrection and eternal life.

Chapter 2 - Doubt of the People

In the story of the raising of Lazarus found in John 11, one of the most striking elements is the Doubt of the People. Even though they had witnessed many of Jesus' miracles and knew of His power, many still doubted His ability to raise Lazarus from the dead. This doubt saddened Jesus and caused Him sorrow because it reflected a lack of faith in who He was and what He had come to do. Even though Jesus had performed countless signs and wonders, including healing the blind and the sick, the people still questioned whether He had the power to overcome death itself. In John 11:37, some of those at Lazarus' tomb expressed this doubt, saying, "Could not this man, which opened the eyes of the blind, have caused that even this man should not have died?" Their words reflected a deep uncertainty about Jesus' authority over death and His ability to reverse its effects. This doubt hurt Jesus because it questioned His power and showed that despite all He had done, people still struggled to believe in Him fully.

The people's doubt is significant because it reflects a broader issue that we all experience in our spiritual lives: the difficulty of trusting God in the face of impossible circumstances. Despite having seen God's faithfulness time and time again, we often find ourselves doubting His power when we are faced with situations that seem beyond hope, like the death of a loved one. The people mourning Lazarus had likely heard about or even witnessed some of the miracles Jesus had performed. They knew that He had healed the blind, the lame, and the sick, yet when it came to death, they questioned whether He had the authority to change the outcome. This doubt came from their inability to fully grasp the extent of Jesus' divine power and His identity as the Son of God. Death, to them, was the ultimate finality, and they could not comprehend how anyone, even someone who had performed great miracles, could undo it.

This doubt deeply moved Jesus because it reflected a fundamental misunderstanding of who He was. Jesus had authority over life and death as the

Son of God, yet the people around Him could not see beyond their immediate circumstances. Their grief and sorrow clouded their faith, and in their minds, once Lazarus had died, there was nothing more that could be done. This reflects how doubt often works in our lives. When faced with difficult or seemingly impossible situations, we tend to focus on the problem rather than God's power to overcome it. Like the people at Lazarus' tomb, we can be so overwhelmed by the situation before us that we forget the miracles we've seen before and question whether God can help us.

What makes this doubt even more painful is the fact that Jesus had explicitly told them that He had the power to raise the dead. Earlier in the chapter, when speaking to Martha, Jesus made a profound statement about His identity, saying, "I am the resurrection, and the life: he that believeth in me, though he were dead, yet shall he live" (John 11:25). Jesus was not only declaring His ability to bring Lazarus back to life, but He was also revealing a more profound truth about His mission and His role in defeating death once and for all. Despite this clear statement, the people still doubted, and their doubt caused Jesus sorrow because it showed that they had not fully understood or embraced His message.

Jesus' sorrow over the people's doubt reminds us how much He longs for us to trust Him fully. He desires us to believe in His power, not just in the small things but in the seemingly impossible. When we doubt, we essentially say that we don't think God can handle our situation or that His power has limits. This doubt grieves God because it reflects a lack of faith in who He is and what He has promised to do. Jesus' weeping at this moment is not just about Lazarus' death but also about the more significant issue of unbelief. He weeps because He sees how deeply ingrained doubt can be in the human heart, even after witnessing His miracles and hearing His teachings.

The doubt of the people also reveals how easy it is for us to forget God's past faithfulness when we are in the midst of a trial. The crowd had likely seen Jesus perform miracles before, yet they still questioned whether He could raise Lazarus from the dead. This is a common human tendency—to forget what God has already done for us when faced with a new challenge. We may have experienced God's provision, healing, or deliverance in the past, but when a new difficulty arises, we often doubt whether He can come through again. This doubt can be extreme in situations that seem final, like death. But Jesus' response to Lazarus' death and the people's doubt shows us that no problem is beyond His power. His authority extends even over death, and He can bring life where there seems to be only loss.

Another aspect of the doubt of the people is that it reflects a limited understanding of Jesus' identity. Many of the people in the crowd likely saw Jesus as a great teacher or healer, but they did not fully grasp that He was the Son of God with authority over all creation, including death. This limited understanding made them question whether He could raise Lazarus from the dead. They had seen Him heal the sick, but they could not imagine He had the power to reverse death. This reflects how our doubts often stem from a limited view of who God is. We do not fully trust God's character or promises when we doubt. We limit God to what we think is possible rather than believing He can do the impossible.

Jesus' response to the people's doubt was not anger or frustration but compassion. He wept because He understood their pain and their struggle to believe. His tears show us that He is patient with us, even when we doubt Him. He understands our weaknesses and difficulties when trying to have faith amid trials. Jesus' weeping reminds us that He is not a distant or cold deity but a compassionate Savior deeply moved by our struggles and doubts. He does not condemn us for our doubts but invites us to bring them to Him so that He can strengthen our faith.

Even though the people doubted, Jesus still performed the miracle of raising Lazarus from the dead. This shows us that God's power does not depend on our faith level. Even when we doubt, God can still work in miraculous ways. Jesus raised Lazarus to demonstrate His power over death and strengthen the faith of those who doubted. In John 11:40, Jesus says to Martha, "Said I not unto thee, that, if thou wouldest believe, thou shouldest see the glory of God?" This statement shows that belief is the key to witnessing the glory of God. Jesus wanted the people to see beyond their doubt and believe in His power so that they could experience the fullness of His glory.

The doubt of the people also serves as a warning for us today. It reminds us of the importance of faith and trust in God, even when faced with hopeless situations. Doubt can prevent us from fully experiencing the power of God in our lives. It can block us from seeing the miracles that God wants to perform. Just as the people doubted Jesus' ability to raise Lazarus, we, too, can find ourselves questioning God's ability to work in our lives. But Jesus' response to their doubt shows He can overcome even impossible situations. He calls us to have faith, to trust in Him, and to believe that He can bring life out of death, hope out of despair, and joy out of sorrow.

In conclusion, the Doubt of the People in John 11 is a powerful lesson about the importance of faith and trust in Jesus. Despite all the miracles they had witnessed, the people still questioned Jesus' ability to raise Lazarus from the dead. Their doubt caused Jesus sorrow because it reflected a lack of faith in His power and His identity as the Son of God. Jesus wept because He longed for them to believe fully in who He was and what He had come to do. His tears show He understands our struggles with doubt and is compassionate toward us even when our faith falters. But Jesus also challenges us to move beyond doubt and to trust in His power, especially in the face of impossible situations. The raising of Lazarus is a reminder that nothing is too complicated for God and that, even amid doubt, Jesus has the power to bring life where there is death and hope where there is despair.

Chapter 3 - Delay in Understanding

In the story of Lazarus from John 11, we encounter a significant moment where Jesus wept, not just because of the death of His dear friend, but because of the Delay in Understanding from the people around Him. Jesus had made it clear on numerous occasions that He was no ordinary man, healer, or prophet but the very Son of God who had power over life and death. However, even those closest to Him—Martha, Mary, and His disciples—struggled to fully grasp the magnitude of His identity as "the resurrection and the life." This delay in understanding caused Jesus deep sorrow, one reason He wept. In John 11:25-26, Jesus said to Martha, "I am the resurrection, and the life: he that believeth in me, though he were dead, yet shall he live: And whosoever liveth and believeth in me shall never die." In these words, Jesus was revealing one of the most profound truths of His ministry—that He had come not only to heal the sick or comfort the grieving but to defeat death itself. Yet, despite His clear statements, the people around Him were still focused on their immediate grief and loss, unable to see beyond their current circumstances to the eternal hope that Jesus was offering. This delay in understanding was a source of sorrow for Jesus because He longed for them to fully comprehend the life-transforming power of His mission.

The delay in understanding the people around Jesus reflects a broader challenge we all face in our spiritual journeys. It can be difficult to see beyond our immediate circumstances, especially when they involve pain, suffering, or loss. Just as Martha and Mary were consumed by their grief over Lazarus' death, we, too, can become so overwhelmed by our struggles that we fail to recognize God's more excellent plan at work. Jesus had repeatedly told His followers that He was the one who had power over life and death, but their sorrow over Lazarus' death closed their eyes to the hope and promise He offered. This is why Jesus wept—not only because of their grief but because they did not yet understand the full extent of who He was and what He had come to accomplish. He wept because He saw how limited their perspective was and desired them to see beyond their immediate circumstances to the eternal life He came to give.

This delay in understanding is something that we can all relate to. In our human experience, it is often difficult to fully trust in God's promises when faced with the harsh realities of life. Just as the people at Lazarus' tomb were fixated on the fact that Lazarus had died, we, too, can become fixated on the problems or challenges in front of us, losing sight of the bigger picture. Jesus had already performed many miracles by this point—He had healed the blind, cured the sick, and even raised others from the dead—yet the people still struggled to believe that He could bring Lazarus back to life after four days in the tomb. Their limited understanding of Jesus' power caused them to doubt what He could do. Jesus' tears in this moment reflect His compassion for our human frailty and our tendency to question, even in the face of His proven faithfulness.

The delay in understanding also points to the broader spiritual blindness many people experience when recognizing who Jesus truly is. Even though Jesus had clearly stated that He was the resurrection and the life, many people still viewed Him through a limited lens, seeing Him as a great teacher or miracle worker but not fully grasping His divine nature. This misunderstanding of Jesus' identity caused Him great sorrow because He knew that without fully understanding who He was, people would not be able to experience the fullness of the life He came to offer. Jesus wanted the people around Him to move beyond their limited understanding and embrace the truth that He was the Son of God, sent to conquer death and bring eternal life to all who believed in Him. His tears were not just for the death of Lazarus but for the spiritual blindness of the people who did not yet see Him for who He indeed was.

This delay in understanding also reveals something important about the nature of faith. Faith is not just about believing in what we can see or understand at the moment; it is about trusting in the promises of God, even when our circumstances suggest otherwise. Martha and Mary believed that Jesus could heal Lazarus while he was still alive, but once he died, their faith wavered. They could not comprehend that Jesus had the power to reverse even death itself. We often experience This delay in understanding in our own lives. We may believe in God's power in some regions of our lives, but when faced with a hopeless situation, we struggle to maintain that faith. Jesus wept because He saw how difficult it was for people to trust Him fully, to believe that He was not just a healer but the very source of life itself.

Jesus' sorrow over the delay in understanding also reflects His desire for us to have a deeper, more intimate relationship with Him. He does not want us to simply view Him as someone who can solve our problems or make our lives easier; He wants us to know Him as the resurrection and the life—the one who has conquered death and offers eternal life to all who believe. This is the core of His mission, and when people fail to understand this, they miss out on the fullness of what He offers. Jesus wept because He longed for the people around Him to see beyond their temporary circumstances and embrace the eternal hope that He came to bring. He wanted them to move from seeing Him as a temporary solution to their immediate problems to recognizing Him as the world's Savior who offers life beyond the grave.

The delay in understanding also teaches us something about Jesus's patience. Even though the people around Him did not fully grasp who He was, Jesus did not give up on them. He did not turn away in frustration or anger; instead, He wept with them, sharing their sorrow and continuing to reveal His power and love. This shows us that Jesus is patient with us, even when we struggle to understand or believe. He knows that our faith is a journey, and He walks with us every step of the way, gently guiding us toward a deeper understanding of who He is. His tears remind us that He is not indifferent to our struggles or doubts; He is compassionate and patient, willing to meet us where we are and help us grow in our faith.

Moreover, Jesus' weeping over the delay in understanding reminds us that He wants us to live with an eternal perspective. The people around Him were focused on the immediate loss of Lazarus, but Jesus was focused on the bigger picture—His mission to bring eternal life to all who believe in Him. This eternal perspective is something that Jesus wants for all of us. He wants us to see beyond the temporary challenges and struggles we face in this life and to trust in the eternal hope that He offers. When our present circumstances consume us, we can quickly lose sight of the greater reality that Jesus has already conquered death and offers us life that will never end. His tears in this moment remind us that He wants us to lift our eyes from our present sorrows and fix our gaze on the eternal life He promised to those who believe in Him.

The delay in understanding also points to the importance of spiritual growth. Martha and Mary had spent time with Jesus; they knew Him personally and saw His miracles. Yet, even with this close relationship, they still struggled to understand His power and purpose fully. This shows us that even those who know Jesus well can experience spiritual growth and understanding delays. But Jesus does not abandon us in our moments of doubt or confusion. Instead, He continues to reveal Himself to us, helping us grow in our understanding of who He is. His weeping over the delay in understanding reminds us that spiritual growth is a process, and Jesus is with us every step of the way, guiding us toward a more profound and fuller knowledge of Him.

In conclusion, the Delay in Understanding that caused Jesus to weep in John 11 is a powerful lesson about the importance of fully grasping who Jesus is and the eternal hope He offers. The people around Jesus, including those who loved Him dearly, struggled to see beyond their immediate grief and loss to the greater reality of Jesus' mission. Their delay in understanding caused Jesus sorrow because He longed for them to move beyond their temporary circumstances and embrace the truth that He is the resurrection and the life. This delay in understanding is something that we all experience in our spiritual journeys. We often find it challenging to trust God's promises when faced with difficult or seemingly hopeless situations. But Jesus' tears remind us that He is patient with us, even in our moments of doubt, and that He desires us to grow in our faith and understanding of who He is. His weeping also challenges us to live with an eternal perspective, trusting in the life and hope that Jesus offers, even in the face of death. Through this story, we are reminded that Jesus is not only the one who comforts us in our grief but also the one who has the power to conquer death and bring eternal life to all who believe in Him. His tears reflect His deep love for us and His desire for us to understand and embrace the life-transforming power of His mission fully

Chapter 4 - Despair of Martha and Mary

In the story of Lazarus found in John 11, the Despair of Martha and Mary is a central element that highlights the depth of their grief and sorrow over the loss of their beloved brother, Lazarus. This moment not only reveals the profound sadness of losing someone they deeply loved but also offers a glimpse into the compassionate and empathetic heart of Jesus. The bond between Jesus and this family was strong, as Lazarus and his sisters Martha and Mary were His dear friends. When Lazarus fell ill, Martha and Mary sent word to Jesus, believing in His ability to heal their brother. Yet, by the time Jesus arrived in Bethany, Lazarus had already died, and their hearts were broken. John 11:32 records the poignant moment when Mary fell at Jesus' feet and said, "Lord, if thou hadst been here, my brother had not died." Her words were a mixture of faith and sorrow, reflecting the anguish she felt as well as her belief that Jesus could have prevented her brother's death. The grief of both sisters was overwhelming, and their sorrow touched the heart of Jesus, leading to one of the most human and compassionate moments in the Gospels—Jesus weeping alongside them.

The despair of Martha and Mary in this passage is not just a reflection of their grief, but it represents the universal experience of loss and the deep sorrow that comes with the death of a loved one. Their reaction is so relatable because it mirrors the feelings that many people experience when faced with death. Martha and Mary had placed their hope in Jesus, believing that He could heal their brother, but now they were confronted with the reality of death, something that seemed final and irreversible. Their despair is palpable, and it reveals the pain of unmet expectations and the sense of abandonment that often accompanies grief. They had hoped that Jesus would come sooner, that He would intervene before it was too late, and when that didn't happen, their sorrow was intensified. Their grief deeply moved Jesus, not because He didn't know what He would do next, but because He empathized with their pain. He felt their heartache and shared in their sorrow, demonstrating His deep compassion for the suffering of those He loved.

What is striking about this moment is that, even though Jesus knew that He would soon raise Lazarus from the dead, He still allowed Himself to feel the weight of the grief around Him. Jesus did not rush past their sorrow or dismiss their pain. Instead, He entered into it, weeping alongside them. His tears reflected His love for Lazarus and His empathy for Martha and Mary. In this moment, Jesus showed that He is not indifferent to human suffering, even though He holds the power to overcome it. His tears demonstrate that He cares deeply about the emotional and physical pain we experience. The fact that Jesus wept knowing that He was about to perform one of the greatest miracles of His ministry, is a powerful reminder that God is with us in our grief, even when He has a plan for redemption and restoration. He doesn't simply look past our pain to the solution; He walks us through it, feeling every tear and heartache.

Martha and Mary's despair is also a reflection of their deep love for their brother, and it reminds us of the intensity of the bonds we share with those we love. Losing someone dear to us brings a level of pain that is difficult to describe. The grief of Martha and Mary was not just about the physical loss of Lazarus but also about the emotional void his absence created. They had shared life, and his death marked the end of that shared journey, leaving them with a profound sense of loss. Their grief was also tied to their faith, as they believed that Jesus could have saved their brother if He had been there. This mixture of faith and sorrow is something that many people experience in times of loss—believing in God's power but wrestling with the pain of loss when things don't happen as they had hoped or prayed. Martha and Mary believed in Jesus, but their understanding of what He could do was limited to what they had seen before healing the sick. They had not yet fully grasped the depth of His power over death itself.

This moment also highlights the compassionate nature of Jesus. His weeping alongside Martha and Mary shows that He doesn't just care about the spiritual aspects of our lives but also the emotional ones. Jesus didn't just come to offer eternal life; He came to bring comfort, hope, and healing to the brokenhearted. In Psalm 34:18, we are reminded, "The Lord is nigh unto them that are of a broken heart; and saveth such as be of a contrite spirit." This verse captures the heart of Jesus in John 11—He was near to Martha and Mary in their brokenness, and His tears reflected His shared sorrow with them. He wasn't distant or detached from their pain. Instead, He was present, weeping alongside them, showing He truly is a God of compassion and love.

The despair of Martha and Mary also speaks to the human tendency to question and doubt in times of suffering. Both sisters believed in Jesus but questioned why He hadn't come sooner. "If thou hadst been here" is a phrase that captures their disappointment and confusion. They believed in Jesus' power but didn't understand why He delayed coming. This is something that many people wrestle with in their faith journeys—why God allows suffering, why He doesn't intervene in the way we expect, and why His timing often seems different from our own. Martha and Mary's questions were not a sign of unbelief but of their deep longing for Jesus to have acted sooner. Their despair was not just about Lazarus' death but also about the seeming silence or absence of Jesus when they needed Him most. Jesus, however, does not rebuke them for their questions. Instead, He meets them in their sorrow and weeps with them, showing that bringing our questions and pain to God is okay. He is not offended by our grief or confusion; He is present with us.

Furthermore, the despair of Martha and Mary highlights the depth of their relationship with Jesus. They didn't just know Him as a distant figure or a healer who performed miracles for strangers. They knew Him personally as a friend. This personal relationship with Jesus made their grief even more intense because they had expected Him to intervene in a way that would spare them from the pain of loss. Their familiarity with Jesus led them to hope for a different outcome, and when that didn't happen, their sorrow was compounded by the feeling that their friend had not come through for them in the way they had hoped. Yet, even in despair, they turned to Jesus, seeking comfort and answers. This shows us that, even in our most profound moments of pain, we can turn to God, trusting He will meet us with compassion and grace.

Ultimately, the despair of Martha and Mary and Jesus' response reveals that God is not indifferent to our suffering. Jesus' tears show that He is deeply moved by the pain we experience. While He has the power to bring resurrection and life, He also feels the weight of death and sorrow. His weeping reminds us that God is not a distant observer of our lives but intimately involved in our struggles and sorrows. Jesus' empathy for Martha and Mary shows us that God is not just concerned with the big picture of salvation but also with the details of our daily lives, including our moments of most profound grief. His tears remind us that He is with us in our suffering, even when we don't fully understand His timing or plans.

In conclusion, the Despair of Martha and Mary in John 11 reveals a profound moment of grief, faith, and compassion. Their sorrow over the loss of their brother Lazarus was a profoundly human response to death, and it touched the heart of Jesus. His weeping alongside them demonstrated His empathy for their pain and His compassion for those He loved. Jesus was not distant or detached from their suffering; He was present with them in their grief, sharing their sorrow. This moment also reminds us that God is with us in our despair. He cares deeply about our emotional and spiritual well-being and meets us with compassion and grace, even when we are overwhelmed by grief. Jesus' tears reflect His deep love for Martha, Mary, and Lazarus and His understanding of the pain that death brings. While Jesus knew that He would raise Lazarus from the dead, He still allowed Himself to feel the moment's weight, showing that He is a God who weeps for us. The story of Lazarus is ultimately one of hope, as Jesus demonstrates His power over death. Still, it is also a story of shared sorrow as Jesus enters into the pain of those He loves, reminding us that He is with us in our grief and offers us the hope of resurrection and eternal life.

Chapter 5 - Divine Compassion

John 11:35, the shortest verse in the Bible, simply says, "Jesus wept." Although the verse is brief, it carries an immense depth of meaning, especially when considering the context of the story of Lazarus. Jesus' tears reflect His Divine Compassion—a profound expression of God's love and care for humanity, especially in the face of suffering and loss. As Jesus stood at the tomb of His friend Lazarus, He was moved to tears, not just for Lazarus or for Martha and Mary, but for all of humanity, for the brokenness of the world, and for the pain that sin and death had brought into God's creation. Jesus' weeping was not just a reaction to the immediate grief of those around Him; it was a powerful demonstration of His divine empathy and compassion for everyone who has ever suffered. In that moment, Jesus, the Son of God, wholly entered into the pain of the human experience, showing us that God is not distant or indifferent to our struggles. His tears reflect His intimate involvement in our lives, His deep care for our well-being, and His desire to comfort us in our darkest moments.

Jesus' tears at the tomb of Lazarus are a reminder that God is a God of compassion. The Greek word used in John 11:33 to describe Jesus' reaction when He saw Mary and the others weeping is often translated as "deeply moved" or "groaned in spirit." This suggests that Jesus felt a deep, emotional stirring as He witnessed the grief of those around Him. He didn't just observe their pain from a distance but entered it. This is a critical aspect of understanding the heart of God. Jesus' tears show us that God is not detached from the world's suffering. Instead, He is deeply involved and cares about the pain we experience. His compassion is not limited to the grand, cosmic scale of saving the world; it is also profoundly personal, reaching down into each person's sorrows and struggles. Jesus wept because He saw the heartache of Mary and Martha, two women who loved their brother dearly and were devastated by his death. He wept because He saw the sadness and confusion of those who had gathered to mourn. But even more than that, Jesus wept because He saw the brokenness of a world that was never meant to experience death.

When Jesus wept, His tears were not just for Lazarus and his family but for all of humanity. He wept because He saw the world's devastating effects of sin and death. From the beginning, God's plan for humanity was one of life, joy, and communion with Him. But when sin entered the world through Adam and Eve's disobedience, death became a reality, and with it came pain, suffering, and sorrow. Romans 5:12 reminds us, "Wherefore, as by one man sin entered into the world, and death by sin; and so death passed upon all men, for that all have sinned." Death was never part of God's original design for creation, and Jesus, knowing this, wept because He saw firsthand the destruction that sin had caused. His tears reflected His sorrow over the broken state of the world, a world that had been marred by sin and was now subject to death. Jesus' weeping at Lazarus' tomb is a reminder that God grieves over the brokenness of creation. He is not a God who is indifferent to the suffering caused by sin; He is a God who cares deeply about the pain that it brings to His people.

At the heart of Jesus' compassion is His profound love for humanity. The love of God is not distant or abstract; it is personal, intimate, and authentic. Jesus' tears show us that God's love is not just a theological concept but a lived reality. He wept because He loved Lazarus, Martha, and Mary, and Their grief moved him. In John 11:36, after Jesus wept, the people said, "Behold how he loved him!" This statement underscores the depth of Jesus' love for His friends, but it also points to a larger truth—Jesus loves each of us with that same deep, compassionate love. His tears are not just for the people in the story of Lazarus; they are for all of us who experience the pain of loss, suffering, and grief. Jesus' weeping reveals that God's love is not just intellectual but emotional and heartfelt. He is not a God who watches from afar as we go through life's difficulties; He is a God who walks with us, feels our pain, and weeps with us in our sorrow.

Moreover, Jesus' tears expressed His identification with the human condition. Jesus fully experienced our emotions, struggles, and pain in His humanity. Hebrews 4:15 tells us, "For we have not an high priest which cannot be touched with the feeling of our infirmities; but was in all points tempted like as we are, yet without sin." Jesus' weeping shows us that He truly understands what it means to be human. He knows what it feels like to lose someone you love.

He knows what it feels like to experience sorrow and heartache. His tears testify that He is not a distant, impersonal deity but a Savior intimately connected to the human experience. Jesus fully entered the human condition as the perfect mediator between God and humanity. His tears at Lazarus' tomb reflect this reality—He came not just to save us from sin but to walk with us in our suffering.

Jesus' tears also reveal His deep empathy for those who are mourning. When He saw Mary, Martha, and the others weeping, He was moved with compassion. His empathy was so strong that He cried with them, even though He knew He would soon raise Lazarus from the dead. This shows us that Jesus' compassion is not just about fixing problems or providing solutions but about being present with people in their pain. Jesus didn't rush past the moment's grief to get to the miracle. He didn't tell Martha and Mary to stop crying because He was about to raise Lazarus. Instead, He paused, entered their sorrow, and wept with them. This is a powerful lesson for us. When we see people in pain, we often want to fix the situation or offer solutions. But sometimes, people need someone to be with them in their grief, weep with them, and share their sorrow. Jesus shows us that genuine compassion is not just about solving problems; it is about entering into the pain of others and walking with them through it.

Another essential aspect of Jesus' weeping is that it points to the heart of the gospel. Jesus came to earth to address the very thing that caused His tears—sin and death. His weeping at Lazarus' tomb foreshadows the more excellent work He would accomplish on the cross. Jesus knew that the only way to address the pain and suffering of the world indeed was to take it upon Himself. His tears reflect His mission to defeat death and bring life. In John 11:25, just before He raised Lazarus, Jesus said to Martha, "I am the resurrection, and the life: he that believeth in me, though he were dead, yet shall he live." This statement reveals the heart of Jesus' mission—He came to bring life, not just physical life, but eternal life. His tears at Lazarus' tomb show us that He was deeply moved by the pain and suffering caused by sin, but they also point to the fact that He came to overcome it. Jesus' weeping is a reminder that while death and suffering are natural, they are not the end of the story. Jesus defeated sin and death through His death and resurrection, offering eternal life to all who believe in Him.

Furthermore, Jesus' compassion is not limited to specific moments of grief or loss. His divine compassion extends to all areas of human suffering—physical pain, emotional heartache, mental struggles, and spiritual brokenness. Jesus cares about every aspect of our lives. His tears at Lazarus' tomb reveal that no part of our pain is too small or insignificant for Him. Whether we are grieving the loss of a loved one, struggling with illness, or feeling overwhelmed by life's challenges, Jesus cares. He sees our pain, and He weeps with us. His compassion is all-encompassing, and His love reaches every corner of our lives. This is a profound comfort for those who are suffering. It means that we are never alone in our pain. Jesus is with us, and He feels our sorrow deeply.

In conclusion, the Divine Compassion of Jesus, as demonstrated in John 11:35, is a powerful reminder of God's love and care for humanity. Jesus wept at the tomb of Lazarus, not just because of the immediate grief of Martha and Mary but because of the larger reality of human suffering and the brokenness of the world caused by sin. His tears reveal the heart of God—a heart that is deeply moved by the pain of His people. Jesus' compassion is not distant or impersonal but intimate, authentic, and deeply felt. He enters our suffering, walks with us in our pain, and offers us the hope of resurrection and eternal life. His tears at Lazarus' tomb reflect His divine love and care for all who suffer, and they remind us that we serve a God who weeps with us, feels our pain, and has the power to bring life out of death. Jesus' compassion is a profound expression of His love for humanity and a source of great comfort for all struggling with grief, loss, or pain. In His tears, we see God's heart full of love, empathy, and the promise of eternal life.

Chapter 6 - Depth of His Humanity

In John 11, when Jesus wept at the tomb of Lazarus, we are given a glimpse into the profound Depth of His Humanity. Though Jesus is fully divine, possessing all the attributes of God, including power over life and death, He is also fully human, experiencing the full range of human emotions and struggles. The fact that Jesus wept, even though He knew He would soon raise Lazarus from the dead, reveals something significant about His character: He was not detached from the realities of human life but deeply connected to the pain and sorrow that come with living in a fallen world. His tears reflected the depth of His humanity, showing that He did not merely observe the suffering of others from a distance but wholly entered into it. He experienced real grief, sadness, and compassion, just as we do. In Hebrews 4:15, we are reminded of this truth: "For we have not an high priest which cannot be touched with the feeling of our infirmities; but was in all points tempted like as we are, yet without sin." This verse highlights that Jesus, in His humanity, experienced the same emotions, struggles, and temptations we face. His weeping at Lazarus' tomb is a powerful demonstration of His empathy and understanding of our deepest emotions. It shows us that He not only understands our pain but feels it with us, providing comfort in the knowledge that we serve a Savior who is fully engaged with the struggles of life.

The depth of Jesus' humanity is most clearly seen in moments like this, where His emotions are fully displayed. He was not immune to grief or unaffected by the sorrow of those around Him. His tears were not just a token gesture or a superficial response to the situation; they were the genuine outpouring of a heart that was moved by the pain of others. Jesus wept because He loved Lazarus, Martha, and Mary and was deeply moved by their grief. His tears show that He is not a distant, detached deity but a Savior walking with us through life's darkest valleys. The fact that Jesus wept, even though He knew He would raise Lazarus from the dead, underscores the reality that human emotions are authentic and valid, even in the context of faith. Jesus knew the situation's outcome, yet He still allowed Himself to feel and express the total weight of sorrow. This teaches us that it is okay to grieve, to feel sadness, and to mourn, even when we have faith in God's power and plan. Jesus' humanity reminds us that emotions are not a sign of weakness but a part of the human experience that even the Son of God embraced.

Jesus' tears also reveal the depth of His compassion for those who suffer. His humanity allowed Him to identify with the pain of others entirely. When He saw Martha and Mary weeping over the loss of their brother, He was deeply moved. He didn't rush past their grief or try to minimize their pain. Instead, He entered into their sorrow, weeping with them. This moment shows us that Jesus doesn't just care about the significant spiritual issues in our lives; He cares about the personal emotional struggles we face every day. He understands what it's like to experience loss, heartache, and grief, and He is present with us in those moments. His tears at the tomb of Lazarus remind us that we are not alone in our pain. Jesus is with us, sharing our sorrow and offering comfort through His presence. His humanity makes Him approachable and relatable, allowing us to come to Him with our deepest hurts, knowing He understands and cares.

Furthermore, the depth of Jesus' humanity is vital to His role as our Savior. To truly save us, Jesus fully entered the human experience. He could not simply remain distant from our struggles; He had to walk through them. By becoming fully human, Jesus could take on the weight of our sins and bear the punishment we deserved. His humanity enabled Him to be the perfect mediator between God and man, bridging the gap that sin had created. In His weeping, we see the heart of a Savior concerned with our eternal salvation and our present suffering. His tears remind us that He is a compassionate and empathetic high priest who understands our weaknesses because He has experienced them. His humanity allows Him to intercede for us with full knowledge of what it means to be human, giving us confidence that He cannot only save us but also comfort and guide us through the trials of life.

The depth of Jesus' humanity is also seen in His willingness to be vulnerable. In a culture where vulnerability is often seen as weakness, Jesus shows us that true strength lies in being willing to feel and express emotions. His tears at Lazarus' tomb are a powerful reminder that vulnerability is not something to be ashamed of but something that connects us to others profoundly. Jesus' willingness to weep with those who were mourning shows us that He was not afraid to be vulnerable, to express His love and compassion in a visible, tangible way. This is a lesson for all of us, as we often feel pressured to hide our emotions or act like we have everything under control. Jesus shows us that it is okay to feel deeply, weep, and express our feelings, especially in the face of loss and suffering. His humanity teaches us that vulnerability is not a sign of weakness but a reflection of our love and compassion for others.

Another critical aspect of the depth of Jesus' humanity is His empathy. Jesus didn't just sympathize with the pain of others; He empathized with them. He didn't just observe their grief from a distance; He entered it, feeling it alongside them. This empathy is what makes Jesus such a compassionate and understanding Savior. He doesn't just know about our struggles intellectually; He has experienced them. When we come to Jesus with our pain, we can be confident that He understands what we are going through because He has felt it Himself. His empathy is one of the most comforting aspects of His humanity. It assures us that we are not alone in our suffering and that Jesus is not indifferent to our pain. His tears at Lazarus' tomb testify that He feels our sorrow as profoundly as we do and is present with us.

The depth of Jesus' humanity is also seen in His ability to relate to the full spectrum of human emotions. Throughout the Gospels, we see Jesus expressing a wide range of emotions—joy, anger, compassion, grief, and even frustration. This reminds us that emotions are a normal and healthy part of being human. Jesus, as the perfect human, experienced all of these emotions without sin, showing us that emotions themselves are not sinful but can reflect our deepest values and relationships. Jesus' weeping at Lazarus' tomb shows us that it is okay to grieve, to feel sadness, and to express our emotions. His humanity teaches us that emotions are not something to be suppressed or ignored but to be embraced and expressed healthily. Jesus' tears remind us that our emotions are a part of who we are as humans and can be a powerful way to connect with others and God.

In addition, Jesus' tears demonstrate the connection between His humanity and His divine mission. Though He was fully human and experienced real emotions, Jesus was also fully divine, and His weeping points to the larger purpose of His mission on earth. Jesus didn't just come to sympathize with our suffering; He came to do something about it. His tears at Lazarus' tomb reflected His deep love for humanity and His desire to defeat the very thing that caused His weeping—death. Jesus knew that His mission was to conquer sin and death through His death and resurrection, and His tears at Lazarus' tomb foreshadowed the ultimate victory He would achieve. His weeping reminds us that while He fully entered the human experience, He also had the power to transform it. Jesus' humanity and divinity were perfectly united in His mission to bring life out of death, and His tears point to the hope of resurrection and eternal life that He came to offer.

Finally, the depth of Jesus' humanity is a source of great comfort for us today. Because Jesus is fully human, He understands our challenges, struggles, and emotions. He knows what it's like to feel sorrow, grief, and pain; He is with us in those moments. His tears at Lazarus' tomb remind us that we do not have a Savior distant or detached from our lives; we have a Savior who fully engages with us, weeps with us, and offers us comfort in our darkest moments. Jesus' humanity assures us we can come to Him with our deepest hurts, knowing He understands and cares. His tears are a powerful reminder that He cannot only save us from sin but also walk us through the trials of life, offering us His presence, compassion, and love.

In conclusion, the Depth of His Humanity is powerfully displayed in Jesus' weeping at the tomb of Lazarus. His tears reveal a Saviour who fully engages with life's struggles, feels the pain and sorrow of the human experience, and is present with us in our suffering. Though He is fully divine, Jesus' humanity allows Him to empathize with our deepest emotions, offering comfort and assurance that we are not alone in our pain. His tears at Lazarus' tomb reflect His deep love for humanity and His desire to bring life out of death. They remind us that Jesus is not only our Savior but also our compassionate and empathetic high priest who walks with us through the darkest valleys of life. His humanity is a source of great comfort and hope, showing us that we serve a God who understands our struggles, weeps with us in our sorrow, and offers us eternal life through His victory over death.

Chapter 7 - Disbelief of the Crowd

In the story of Lazarus, found in John 11, one of the most poignant themes is the Disbelief of the Crowd. This disbelief runs as a steady undercurrent throughout the narrative, impacting Jesus profoundly, to the point that He wept not only for the death of Lazarus but also for the failure of those around Him to trust and believe in His power over death fully. The crowd gathered to mourn Lazarus' death exhibited a mix of belief and disbelief. Some had heard of or witnessed Jesus' previous miracles and believed in His healing ability. In contrast, others were skeptical, doubting His power and authority, particularly in the face of death. This doubt is exemplified in John 11:40, where Jesus said, "Said I not unto thee, that, if thou wouldest believe, thou shouldest see the glory of God?" This statement captures Jesus' sadness and frustration with the people's inability to see beyond their immediate circumstances and trust in His identity and mission. It highlights that belief, or rather the lack thereof, was one of the central issues at play.

The crowd's limited understanding of who Jesus was at the heart of this disbelief. Many people viewed Him as a healer, a teacher, and perhaps a prophet, but few fully grasped His divine nature as the Son of God. They had seen Him heal the sick and perform miraculous signs, but death, in their minds, was a final and insurmountable obstacle. Their belief in Jesus' power stopped at the point of death, and this was the source of their doubt. They believed that if Jesus had arrived earlier, He could have healed Lazarus and prevented his death, but now that Lazarus had died, they saw no hope. This limited understanding of Jesus' identity grieved Him because He had come not only to heal the sick but to defeat death itself. His mission was to offer eternal life, to show that death was not the final word, yet the crowd could not see past their immediate grief to understand the greater reality of who He was and what He had come to do.

This disbelief was intellectual, profoundly emotional, and rooted in fear and sorrow. The people were consumed by their grief, and in their sorrow, they lost sight of Jesus' power and authority. It is a typical human response to overwhelming circumstances—when faced with loss, pain, or seemingly impossible problems, it can be difficult to maintain faith. The crowd's disbelief reflects the challenge of holding onto faith when everything seems hopeless. They had placed their hope in Jesus while Lazarus was alive, but when he died, their hope seemed to die with him. Jesus wept, not just for Lazarus, but for the disbelief that surrounded Him, for the people who could not see beyond the darkness of their grief to the light of His glory.

What makes this disbelief even more heartbreaking is that Jesus had already revealed His power and authority over life and death. In John 11:25-26, He had told Martha, "I am the resurrection, and the life: he that believeth in me, though he were dead, yet shall he live: And whosoever liveth and believeth in me shall never die." This was a bold and explicit declaration of Jesus' divine identity and His power over death. Yet even with this revelation, the people struggled to believe. Their disbelief was not just a failure to understand intellectually but a more profound spiritual blindness that prevented them from seeing the fullness of who Jesus was. This spiritual blindness is something that Jesus encountered throughout His ministry. Time and again, He performed miracles, taught with authority, and revealed His identity as the Son of God, but many people, including those closest to Him, still struggled to believe.

The disbelief of the crowd reflects the broader struggle of humanity to fully trust in God's power, especially in the face of death. Death is the great equalizer, the one thing that no human can escape or control, and it brings with it a sense of finality that can overwhelm even the most vigorous faith. The crowd at Lazarus' tomb had seen Jesus heal the sick and perform miracles, but death seemed like an insurmountable barrier. This disbelief highlights a common human tendency to place limits on what we believe God can do. We may trust God in certain areas of our lives, but when faced with a situation as final and irreversible as death, our faith can falter. Jesus wept because He saw this lack of faith and inability to trust in His power over death fully, and it deeply saddened Him. He longed for the people to believe, see beyond the immediate reality of Lazarus' death, and trust in His divine mission's more significant reality.

Jesus' weeping over the crowd's disbelief reveals His compassion for human weakness. He understood the fear and sorrow the people were experiencing and did not rebuke them harshly for their lack of faith. Instead, He wept with them, sharing in their grief and their struggle to believe. His tears show us that God is not indifferent to our doubts and struggles. He understands that faith can be difficult, especially in the face of overwhelming circumstances, and He meets us in our doubt with compassion and grace. Jesus' tears remind us that He is patient with us, even when we struggle to believe. He doesn't turn away from us in our moments of doubt; instead, He draws near to us, offering His presence and comfort as we wrestle with our faith.

Another critical aspect of the crowd's disbelief is that it serves as a warning for us today. It challenges us to examine our faith and to ask ourselves whether we truly believe in the power of Jesus, even in the most challenging and hopeless situations. The crowd's disbelief was not just about Lazarus; it was about their inability to trust in Jesus' identity and His mission fully. They believed in Him up to a certain point, but when faced with death, their faith faltered. This is a challenge for all of us. Do we trust Jesus only when things are going well, or do we believe in His power even in the face of death, loss, and despair? The crowd's disbelief reminds us that faith is not just about believing in God's power when it is easy but about trusting Him even when everything seems hopeless.

The crowd's disbelief also points to the tension between faith and sight. The people who witnessed Lazarus' death were focused on what they could see—the cold, hard reality of the tomb. They saw death as final and irreversible, and because of this, they struggled to believe in the possibility of resurrection. This tension between faith and sight is something that Jesus often addressed in His ministry. In John 20:29, Jesus said to Thomas after His resurrection, "Blessed are they that have not seen, and yet have believed." Faith, by its very nature, requires us to trust what we cannot see and believe in God's power even when our circumstances contradict it. The crowd at Lazarus' tomb was so focused on what they could see—the death of Lazarus—that they could not see the greater reality of Jesus' power to bring life out of death.

Jesus' response to the disbelief of the crowd is also significant. Instead of chastising them for their lack of faith, He performed one of His greatest miracles—raising Lazarus from the dead. This miracle was not just about bringing Lazarus back to life; it was a demonstration of Jesus' power over death and a sign of His identity as the Son of God. In John 11:40, Jesus said, "Said I not unto thee, that, if thou wouldest believe, thou shouldest see the glory of God?" This statement reveals that belief is the key to seeing the glory of God. Jesus wanted the crowd to understand that their faith, or lack of it, directly impacted their ability to witness the fullness of His power. Jesus gave them a tangible demonstration of His power by raising Lazarus from the dead. Still, He also called them to a deeper faith that would go beyond the physical miracle and recognize Him as the resurrection and the life.

In conclusion, the Disbelief of the Crowd in John 11 is a powerful lesson about the challenges of faith and the importance of trusting in Jesus, even in the face of death. The crowd that gathered to mourn Lazarus exhibited a mix of belief and disbelief, struggling to trust in Jesus' power and authority over death fully. This disbelief saddened Jesus, reflecting a lack of faith in His identity and mission. Even though He had revealed Himself as the resurrection and the life, the people were still focused on their immediate circumstances and could not see beyond the reality of death. Jesus' weeping over their disbelief shows us His deep compassion for human weakness and His desire for us to trust in Him fully. His tears remind us that God is patient with us, even when we struggle to believe, and that He meets us in our doubt with grace and compassion. The crowd's disbelief also serves as a challenge for us today, calling us to examine our faith and to trust in Jesus' power, even in the most hopeless situations. Ultimately, Jesus' response to the crowd's disbelief—raising Lazarus from the dead—demonstrates His power over death and His desire for us to see the glory of God through faith. His tears and actions remind us that while faith can be difficult, especially in the face of death, it is through faith that we can witness the fullness of God's power and experience the hope of resurrection and eternal life.

Chapter 8 - Defeat of Sin and Death

In John 11, we witness Jesus weeping at the tomb of Lazarus, and His tears hold profound significance. One of the critical reasons Jesus wept was because He understood the Defeat of Sin and Death that He was about to accomplish. Still, He also profoundly felt the devastating consequences of sin, which had brought death into the world. His tears were not just for Lazarus, Mary, or Martha but for all of humanity and the brokenness caused by sin. From the very beginning, when Adam and Eve disobeyed God in the Garden of Eden, sin entered the world and, with it, death. As Romans 6:23 states, "For the wages of sin is death; but the gift of God is eternal life through Jesus Christ our Lord." Death, both physical and spiritual, is the ultimate consequence of sin. It separates people from God, brings pain and sorrow, and represents the broken state of a once-perfect world. Jesus, as the Son of God, knew all of this, and when He stood before Lazarus' tomb, His tears reflected not only His grief but also His sorrow over the entire human condition. He wept because He saw the deep chasm that sin had created between God and humanity, and He knew that death was the painful outcome of that separation.

Jesus felt the total weight of the world's brokenness at that moment. He was not just mourning the loss of a friend; He was mourning the broken relationship between God and humanity, a relationship that had been damaged by sin and resulted in death. Every death, every moment of grief and suffering, is a reminder of the fall of humanity and the far-reaching consequences of sin. Jesus wept because He knew that sin had corrupted the world, leading to death, disease, and suffering, things that were never part of God's original plan. God created humanity to live in perfect harmony with Him, free from the curse of death, but sin brought about the complete opposite. Death became a harsh reality, and it permeates all aspects of life, bringing pain, sorrow, and separation. As Jesus stood before Lazarus' tomb, He wept over this reality, fully aware of the devastation sin had caused and the toll it had taken on the people He loved.

Jesus' tears also reflect His deep compassion for the human experience of suffering and death. Even though He knew that He would raise Lazarus from the dead, He still allowed Himself to feel and express the moment's sorrow. This is a powerful reminder that God is not indifferent to our suffering. Jesus, fully human and fully divine, experienced the full range of human emotions, including grief, sorrow, and pain. He didn't just observe the suffering of others from a distance; He entered into it, sharing in the heartbreak and loss that comes with death. His tears show us that God is not detached from our struggles. He sees our pain, and He feels it deeply. Jesus' weeping reminds us that God cares about the suffering caused by sin and death and longs to bring comfort and healing to a broken world. His tears reflect His empathy and His desire to restore what has been lost because of sin.

However, Jesus' tears were not just a reflection of sorrow but also a foreshadowing of His ultimate victory over sin and death. Even as He wept, Jesus knew He was about to raise Lazarus from the dead, demonstrating His power over death and giving a glimpse of the resurrection. But more importantly, He knew that shortly, He would defeat death through His death and resurrection. The cross was looming, and Jesus understood that it was the only way to break the power of sin and death over humanity. Therefore, his tears at Lazarus' tomb were for the present and future. He wept because He knew the cost of defeating death would be His own life. Jesus would have to face death head-on, carrying the weight of the world's sin upon His shoulders, to bring eternal life to all who believe in Him. His tears reflected the heavy burden He bore as the Savior of the world, but they also pointed to the hope of the resurrection and the defeat of death that He would soon accomplish.

The significance of Jesus' defeat of sin and death cannot be overstated. From the moment sin entered the world, death became a reality for all of humanity. It is the great enemy no one can escape, representing the ultimate separation from God. But through His death and resurrection, Jesus conquered death, offering eternal life to all who put their faith in Him. As Romans 6:23 reminds us, while the wages of sin is death, the gift of God is eternal life through Jesus Christ. Jesus' tears at Lazarus' tomb remind us of the cost of that gift—the suffering, the sacrifice, and the victory He achieved on our behalf. His tears were not just for the moment but for the entire human condition and the redemption He was about to bring. By raising Lazarus from the dead, Jesus previewed what was to come—His resurrection, which would offer hope and life to all who believe.

Jesus' weeping also serves as a reminder that while death has been defeated, its effects are still felt today. Sin continues to cause pain, suffering, and death, and we still live in a world that is broken. But because of Jesus' victory over death, we have hope. His tears remind us that God is not blind to the suffering we endure, but they also remind us that this suffering is not the end of the story. Jesus' resurrection ensures that death does not have the final word. For those who believe in Him, death is not a permanent state but a transition into eternal life. Jesus' weeping at Lazarus' tomb points us to this greater reality—while death is painful and natural, it is not the end. Through Jesus, we have the promise of resurrection and eternal life with God, free from the curse of sin and death.

Moreover, Jesus' defeat of sin and death offers us a new way of living in the present. Because He has conquered death, we are no longer bound by the fear of death or the consequences of sin. Through faith in Jesus, we are set free from the power of sin, and we can live in the hope of eternal life. Jesus' weeping shows us His deep concern for the consequences of sin, but His resurrection shows us that He has the power to overcome it. This victory empowers us to live lives of faith, hope, and love, knowing that death is not the end and that we have been given the gift of eternal life through Jesus Christ. His tears remind us of the world's brokenness, but His resurrection reminds us that God is making everything new.

In conclusion, the Defeat of Sin and Death is at the heart of why Jesus wept at the tomb of Lazarus. His tears were not only for Lazarus and his family but all of humanity and the brokenness caused by sin. Jesus wept because He felt the weight of the world's suffering, knowing that death was the ultimate consequence of sin. Yet even as He wept, He knew He was about to defeat death through His resurrection. His tears reflect His deep compassion for those who suffer and His determination to bring life and hope to a broken world. Jesus' victory over sin and death is the cornerstone of the Christian faith, offering eternal life to all who believe in Him. His tears at Lazarus' tomb remind us of the cost of that victory—the suffering and sacrifice He endured on our behalf—but they also point us to the hope of resurrection and eternal life. Through His death and resurrection, Jesus has defeated death, and because of that, we can live in the assurance that death is not the end, and eternal life is the gift that awaits all who trust in Him.

Chapter 9 - Desire for Restoration

In John 11, when Jesus wept at the tomb of Lazarus, His tears reflected not only the immediate grief of the moment but also His profound Desire for Restoration. Jesus' weeping often expresses His empathy and compassion for Lazarus' family and friends. Still, it also points to a more profound longing within Jesus to fully restore all things. Though He was about to raise Lazarus from the dead, Jesus understood that this miracle was only temporary. Lazarus would live again, but the world would still be under the curse of sin, and death would continue to reign. Jesus' tears were not just for Lazarus, Martha, and Mary but for all of humanity. They were for a broken world that continued to suffer under the weight of sin and death. His weeping in that moment reflects His deep desire to see the world restored to its original state—free from death, pain, and sorrow. This desire for restoration is echoed in Revelation 21:4, where we are given a glimpse of God's ultimate plan for the future: "And God shall wipe away all tears from their eyes; and there shall be no more death, neither sorrow, nor crying, neither shall there be any more pain: for the former things are passed away." Jesus longed for this day when all things would be made new, and His tears at Lazarus' tomb were a sign of His yearning for that final restoration.

The moment when Jesus wept highlights the tension between the "already" and the "not yet" of God's kingdom. Jesus had already come into the world to bring salvation, and His miracles, including the raising of Lazarus, were signs of the kingdom breaking into the present. Yet, the fullness of that kingdom—the complete restoration of all things—had not yet arrived. Jesus knew that while He had the power to raise Lazarus from the dead, death would still have its hold on the world for a time. The raising of Lazarus was a temporary victory, a foretaste of the more excellent victory that Jesus would accomplish through His death and resurrection. But even as He prepared to perform this incredible miracle, Jesus wept because He knew that the complete restoration of creation would only come through His sacrifice on the cross. His tears, then, were not just an expression of grief for the present moment but a reflection of His sorrow over the ongoing reality of sin and death in the world.

Jesus' desire for restoration goes beyond the physical realm. While the resurrection of Lazarus was a physical demonstration of His power over death, Jesus' ultimate mission was to bring about a spiritual restoration that would affect all of creation. The world was not only physically broken by sin but also spiritually separated from God. Jesus longed to heal that separation and restore the relationship between God and humanity fractured by sin. His tears at Lazarus' tomb reflect His deep longing for the day when that separation would be no more, when humanity would be fully reconciled to God, and the curse of sin would be lifted. This restoration would not come through a single miracle but through the redemptive work that Jesus would accomplish on the cross. By taking on the world's sin and dying in our place, Jesus made way for the restoration of all physical and spiritual things. His tears showed His deep commitment to this mission, even as He prepared to raise Lazarus from the dead.

His deep compassion for humanity is at the heart of Jesus' desire for restoration. Throughout His ministry, Jesus demonstrated over and over again that He cared deeply about the suffering of the people He encountered. He healed the sick, gave sight to the blind, fed the hungry, and raised the dead—all acts of compassion pointing to God's kingdom's coming restoration. But Jesus knew that these acts of healing, while necessary, were not the final solution to the problem of sin and death. His tears at Lazarus' tomb reflect His understanding that the world needed more than temporary fixes; it required a complete restoration that would only be possible through His sacrificial death and resurrection. Jesus' compassion for the suffering of humanity was not limited to individual acts of healing. He longed for a world where suffering, death, and sin would be no more—a world that would only come to pass through His victory over the grave.

In Revelation 21:4, we are given a vision of the future restoration that Jesus longed for: "And God shall wipe away all tears from their eyes; and there shall be no more death, neither sorrow, nor crying, neither shall there be any more pain: for the former things are passed away." This passage gives us a glimpse of the ultimate hope that Jesus pointed to in His ministry. His tears at Lazarus' tomb were not just for the immediate loss of His friend; they were for the entire human condition. Jesus wept because He saw the pain, suffering, and death that sin had brought into the world, and He longed for the day when all of that would be wiped away. The raising of Lazarus was a temporary victory over death, but it pointed to the more incredible victory that Jesus would achieve through His resurrection. In that moment, Jesus' tears reflected His desire for the final restoration of all things, a day when death would be defeated.

Jesus' weeping at Lazarus' tomb also shows us that He was not detached from the struggles of life. Even though He knew that He would raise Lazarus from the dead, He still allowed Himself to feel the pain and sorrow of the moment. His tears are a powerful reminder that Jesus fully engages with the world's suffering. He is not a distant or detached Savior; He is present with us in our pain and feels the weight of the brokenness that sin has brought into the world. But His tears also point to the hope of restoration. Jesus' desire for restoration is not just about healing the physical wounds of the world; it is about bringing a complete and final end to suffering, death, and sin. His tears remind us that while we may experience pain and sorrow in this life, there is a future hope—a day when God will wipe away every tear and make all things new.

The restoration that Jesus longed for is not just a future reality; it begins now, in the present. Through His death and resurrection, Jesus has already started the work of restoring creation. Those who believe in Him are given new life, and the promise of eternal life is made available to all who believe. But while the restoration has begun, it is not yet complete. We still live in a world that is broken by sin, and we still experience the pain and sorrow that comes with that brokenness. Jesus' tears at Lazarus' tomb remind us that He understands the tension we live in—the "already" and the "not yet" of the kingdom of God. His tears point us to the future hope of restoration but also assure us that He is with us in the present, comforting us in our pain and sorrow as we wait for the day when all things will be made new.

The ultimate restoration that Jesus longed for is a world without death, sorrow, and suffering. This is the hope that we cling to as followers of Christ. His tears at Lazarus' tomb remind us that while we may experience moments of grief and loss in this life, they are not the end of the story. Jesus' victory over death through His resurrection ensures that all things will be restored one day. The curse of sin will be lifted, and we will live in perfect harmony with God, free from the pain and sorrow that sin has brought into the world. Jesus' weeping in John

11 points us to this greater reality, reminding us that while death may still sting for now, it will not have the final word. The restoration that Jesus desires is for individuals and the entire creation. In Revelation 21:5, God declares, "Behold, I make all things new." This is the restoration that Jesus wept for—the renewal of all creation, where death, sin, and suffering will be no more.

In conclusion, Jesus' weeping at the tomb of Lazarus reflects His Desire for Restoration. This restoration goes beyond the immediate resurrection of Lazarus and points to the ultimate restoration of all things. Jesus wept not only for the loss of His friend but for the brokenness of the world caused by sin. His tears reflected His deep compassion for humanity and His longing for the day when death and sorrow would be no more. While He knew that He would raise Lazarus from the dead, He also knew that the complete restoration of creation would only come through His sacrificial death and resurrection. Jesus' tears remind us that God is not indifferent to our suffering. He feels the weight of the brokenness in the world and longs for the day when all things will be made new. But His tears also point us to the hope of restoration—a day when God will wipe away every tear, and death will be defeated once and for all. Through His death and resurrection, Jesus has already begun the work of restoration. While we wait for the final fulfillment of that promise, we can find comfort in the knowledge that He is with us, sharing in our pain and pointing us to the hope of a future where all things will be made new.

Chapter 10 - Display of God's Power

In John 11, the story of Lazarus' death and resurrection profoundly illustrates Jesus' deep humanity and His divine authority, culminating in a stunning Display of God's Power. While the miracle of raising Lazarus from the dead is central to the narrative, the tears Jesus shed before performing the miracle hold significant meaning. These tears were not a sign of weakness, nor did they reflect any doubt about the miracle He was about to perform. Instead, Jesus wept to show that God's power and love are intertwined and that His authority over life and death is exercised with deep compassion and empathy for the human condition. In John 11:41-42, we read, "And Jesus lifted up his eyes, and said, Father, I thank thee that thou hast heard me. And I knew that thou hearest me always." These verses reveal Jesus' intimate relationship with the Father and His absolute confidence in the divine power that He was about to demonstrate. Yet, despite knowing the outcome, Jesus allowed Himself to experience the total weight of grief, showing that His emotional involvement in the miracle was as significant as the miracle itself. His tears reflected His compassion for those who mourned Lazarus and His deep understanding of the brokenness and suffering caused by sin and death.

Jesus' tears, combined with the miracle of Lazarus' resurrection, provide a powerful testimony to the nature of God's power. Often, power is associated with force, control, or authority that is detached and unemotional. However, Jesus' weeping shows that God's power is not cold or indifferent but deeply personal and compassionate. The tears that Jesus shed before raising Lazarus illustrate that God's power works through love and empathy, reaching into the depths of human sorrow to bring hope, healing, and restoration. By weeping, Jesus demonstrated that He was not merely a distant figure wielding divine authority but fully engaged in the pain and suffering of the people He loved. His tears were a sign that God's power is not just about the miraculous act of raising the dead but also about entering into the human experience of grief and loss, sharing our pain, and offering comfort in suffering.

The fact that Jesus wept, even though He knew He would raise Lazarus from the dead, underscores the depth of His emotional connection to the situation. This connection was with Lazarus and his family and with all of humanity, as Jesus felt the weight of the brokenness that sin had brought into the world. His tears were a response to the reality of death and the pain it caused, but they also pointed to the greater truth that He had come to conquer death and bring eternal life. Jesus' weeping was not a contradiction to His power but an integral part of it, showing that His authority over life and death was not detached from the human experience. Instead, it was rooted in His deep love for humanity and His desire to bring life where there had been death. The tears He shed were a prelude to the demonstration of God's ultimate power—the power to defeat death and offer new life.

When Jesus raised Lazarus from the dead, it was not merely an isolated miracle but a sign pointing to His divine mission to defeat death once and for all. The raising of Lazarus was a foreshadowing of Jesus' death and resurrection, through which He would conquer the power of sin and death for all time. In this moment, Jesus displayed God's power over death and revealed His identity as the Son of God, the one who holds the keys to life and death. By calling Lazarus out of the tomb, Jesus declared that death does not have the final word. His tears, therefore, were not just for the momentary grief of losing a friend but for the larger reality of death's hold on humanity—a hold that He was about to break through His death and resurrection.

In John 11:41-42, Jesus' prayer before raising Lazarus reveals His deep connection with the Father and His confidence in the power that would be displayed. "Father, I thank thee that thou hast heard me. And I knew that thou hearest me always." This prayer shows that Jesus did not doubt the outcome of the miracle. He knew that Lazarus would rise again, and He prayed aloud so that those around Him could witness the power of God and believe. Jesus wanted the crowd to see that the miracle was not just an act of compassion but a demonstration of divine authority. His tears, therefore, were not a sign of uncertainty but a reflection of His deep empathy for the people around Him and the world's brokenness. Jesus wept because He understood the pain that death causes and wanted those around Him to know that God's power is not distant or abstract but deeply involved in the human experience.

The combination of Jesus' weeping and His raising of Lazarus shows that God's power is not only about the ability to perform miracles but also about entering into our suffering and bringing redemption. Jesus did not perform the miracle of raising Lazarus in a detached or emotionless way; He was fully engaged with the people around Him, sharing in their grief and offering them hope. This demonstrates that God's power is not simply about fixing problems or reversing the effects of death; it is about restoring relationships, healing hearts, and bringing wholeness to a broken world. Jesus' tears show that He is not indifferent to our suffering. He cares deeply about the pain we experience, and His power works through that compassion to bring about transformation.

The raising of Lazarus also serves as a potent reminder that God's power is not limited by the constraints of time or human understanding. Lazarus had been dead for four days, and in the minds of those around him, there was no hope of his return. But Jesus' power transcends human limitations. His tears, combined with His command for Lazarus to come forth, demonstrate that God's power is not confined by what we think is possible. Jesus was not limited by the fact that Lazarus had been dead for days; His power extended beyond the grave, showing that God's authority over life and death is absolute. The crowd, who had initially doubted Jesus' ability to raise Lazarus, witnessed firsthand the display of God's power, and many believed as a result. Jesus' weeping, therefore, was not just an emotional response to the situation; it was a profound demonstration of God's love and power working together to bring life out of death.

Furthermore, Jesus' tears and His raising of Lazarus point to the hope of the resurrection for all who believe in Him. While Lazarus' resurrection was a temporary return to life, it foreshadowed the eternal life that Jesus offers to all who put their faith in Him. Jesus' tears remind us that God understands the pain of death, but His power shows us that death is not the end. Through His own death and resurrection, Jesus would offer eternal life to all who believe, conquering the power of death once and for all. The raising of Lazarus was a sign of this greater victory, and Jesus' tears reflected His compassion for a world that was still waiting for the fullness of that victory to be realized.

In conclusion, the Display of God's Power in the raising of Lazarus is a profound demonstration of both Jesus' divine authority and His deep compassion for humanity. Jesus wept not out of weakness or uncertainty but out of empathy for the suffering caused by death. His tears revealed His emotional involvement in the miracle and His desire to show that God's power is not distant or detached but deeply connected to the human experience. By raising Lazarus from the dead, Jesus demonstrated that God's power is greater than death and that His love is woven into every act of His divine authority. The tears that Jesus shed reflected His deep love for humanity and His desire to bring life where there had been death. This miracle was not only a temporary victory over death but a foreshadowing of the ultimate victory that Jesus would accomplish through His own death and resurrection. Through this act, Jesus revealed the nature of God's power—compassionate, personal, and transformative—showing that God is not only able to conquer death but also willing to enter into our pain and bring us the hope of eternal life.

Chapter 11 - Defensive Against Unbelief

In the story of Lazarus, Jesus' weeping serves not only as a powerful display of compassion and empathy but also as a form of Defensive Against Unbelief. His tears, often interpreted as expressions of sorrow for Lazarus' death and empathy for Martha and Mary's grief, carried a deeper significance in the context of the unbelief that surrounded Him. Many who were present during this event doubted Jesus' power, despite witnessing or hearing about His previous miracles. The emotional depth of His reaction to Lazarus' death was, in part, a response to the hardened hearts of those who refused to believe in His ability to conquer death. In Mark 6:6, we read about how Jesus "marveled because of their unbelief. And he went round about the villages, teaching." This verse captures the profound impact that unbelief had on Jesus throughout His ministry. Time and time again, He encountered people who, despite witnessing His miracles and hearing His teachings, remained skeptical of His divine authority. Jesus' tears at Lazarus' tomb reflected His deep sorrow not only for the death of His friend but also for the stubbornness of those who doubted Him, even as He prepared to perform one of the most miraculous acts of His earthly ministry.

Unbelief is a recurring theme in the Gospels, and it is often met with Jesus' frustration or sadness. Throughout His ministry, Jesus performed countless miracles—healing the sick, giving sight to the blind, calming storms, and even raising the dead—yet many still refused to believe that He was the Messiah, the Son of God. In the case of Lazarus, Jesus had already demonstrated His power and authority over life and death by raising others, yet the people surrounding Him still doubted. Their disbelief was not just a rejection of His ability to perform miracles; it was a rejection of His identity as the Savior of the world. Jesus' weeping, therefore, was not only an expression of sorrow for the immediate situation but also a rebuke to those who, despite all they had seen and heard, continued to doubt Him.

The people's skepticism was deeply troubling to Jesus because unbelief is not merely an intellectual stance; it is a spiritual condition that hardens the heart against the truth of God's power and love. Jesus had already told Martha, "I am the resurrection and the life: he that believeth in me, though he were dead, yet shall he live" (John 11:25). This was a clear and direct statement of His divine authority over death, yet many still did not believe. Their unbelief was not based on a lack of evidence; rather, it stemmed from a refusal to accept Jesus for who He truly was. Jesus wept because He knew that their disbelief would keep them from experiencing the fullness of God's power and the eternal life that He offered. His tears were a defense against the hardened hearts that refused to acknowledge His divine nature, and they served as a rebuke to the spiritual blindness that kept people from seeing the truth.

Jesus' weeping in the face of unbelief also demonstrates the emotional toll that such stubbornness took on Him. Throughout His ministry, Jesus encountered both belief and unbelief, and while He rejoiced in the faith of those who trusted Him, He was often deeply saddened by those who rejected Him. In Mark 6:6, we see a clear example of this: "And he marveled because of their unbelief." This verse captures the astonishment and sorrow that Jesus felt when people, despite all the evidence, refused to believe in Him. His tears at Lazarus' tomb reflect a similar emotional response. Jesus was not indifferent to the disbelief of those around Him; He was deeply moved by it, and His tears reflected His desire for people to open their hearts and believe in the power and love of God.

The unbelief of the crowd around Lazarus' tomb was not just a rejection of Jesus' power to raise the dead; it was a rejection of the hope and life that He came to bring. Jesus had come into the world to offer eternal life, to defeat sin and death, and to reconcile humanity with God. His mission was one of restoration and redemption, yet many people, blinded by their skepticism, refused to accept the gift He offered. Jesus' tears were a response to this spiritual blindness. He wept not only for the physical death of Lazarus but also for the spiritual death that unbelief brings. Unbelief cuts people off from the life and hope that Jesus offers, and this was a source of deep sorrow for Him. His tears were a defense against the unbelief that kept people from experiencing the fullness of God's love and power.

Furthermore, Jesus' weeping in the face of unbelief was a call to those around Him to reconsider their doubts and open their hearts to faith. His tears were not just an expression of sorrow; they were a challenge to the crowd to see beyond their skepticism and recognize the divine power that was about to be displayed. Jesus knew that raising Lazarus from the dead would be a powerful demonstration of God's authority over life and death, but He also knew that this miracle alone would not be enough to convince some people. True belief requires more than witnessing a miracle; it requires a heart that is open to the truth of who Jesus is. Jesus wept because He saw the hardness of the hearts around Him, and His tears were a plea for people to soften their hearts and believe in the power of God.

Unbelief is a powerful force that can blind people to the truth, even when that truth is standing right in front of them. The people who doubted Jesus at Lazarus' tomb were not strangers to His miracles. Many of them had likely seen or heard of the healings and other miraculous signs that Jesus had performed. Yet, when confronted with the reality of death, their faith faltered. They could not imagine that Jesus had the power to reverse death, even though He had already demonstrated His authority over sickness and disease. Their unbelief reflected the human tendency to place limits on God's power, to believe in His ability to act up to a certain point but to doubt when the situation seems impossible. Jesus wept because He saw this limitation in their faith, and His tears were a response to the deep frustration and sorrow that comes from witnessing people doubt the very thing He came to reveal—God's power to bring life out of death.

The unbelief that Jesus encountered at Lazarus' tomb is not unique to that moment in history. It reflects the ongoing struggle that people have with faith. Even today, many people wrestle with doubts about God's power and love, particularly in the face of suffering, death, and other challenges. Jesus' weeping reminds us that God is not indifferent to our struggles with unbelief. He understands the difficulties we face in trusting Him, and He is deeply moved by the spiritual blindness that keeps people from experiencing His love and grace. His tears are a reminder that unbelief is not just a rejection of intellectual facts; it is a rejection of the relationship that God desires to have with us. Jesus longs for people to believe in Him, not just because of the miracles He can perform but because of the eternal life and hope that He offers.

In conclusion, Jesus' weeping at Lazarus' tomb was not only an expression of His sorrow for the death of His friend but also a Defensive Against Unbelief. His tears were a response to the hardened hearts of those who refused to believe in His power and divine authority. Despite having performed many miracles, Jesus was continually met with skepticism and doubt, and His weeping reflected the deep emotional toll that this unbelief took on Him. He marveled at their unbelief, just as He had in other moments of His ministry, and His tears served as a rebuke to the spiritual blindness that kept people from seeing the truth. Jesus wept because He saw the devastating impact that unbelief has on people's lives—it cuts them off from the life and hope that God offers. His tears were not just for the immediate grief of losing Lazarus but for the larger reality of spiritual death that comes from unbelief. Through His tears, Jesus called the crowd to reconsider their doubts and open their hearts to faith, showing that God's power is not only about performing miracles but also about transforming hearts and minds. His weeping stands as a defense against the unbelief that keeps people from experiencing the fullness of God's love, urging us to trust in His power and believe in the life that He offers.

Chapter 12 - Demonstration of His Love

In John 11, when Jesus stood at the tomb of His dear friend Lazarus and wept, His tears served as a profound Demonstration of His Love for Lazarus, as well as for Lazarus' sisters, Mary and Martha. This moment is one of the most personal and intimate displays of Jesus' humanity and His deep affection for those He cherished. The grief and sorrow of losing a loved one is a universal experience, and in this instance, Jesus entered fully into that pain, showing that His love is not distant or abstract but deeply personal and relational. In John 11:36, the people who witnessed this moment exclaimed, "Behold how he loved him!" They recognized in Jesus' tears a profound and genuine love, one that went beyond the display of miracles and power. His weeping showed His personal investment in the lives of those He cared for and His heartfelt compassion for their suffering. Jesus' tears were not just a reaction to the death of Lazarus; they were a revelation of His character—He is a God who loves deeply, feels our pain, and is personally involved in our lives.

The fact that Jesus wept, despite knowing that He would soon raise Lazarus from the dead, reveals the depth of His love. Jesus, being fully divine, knew the outcome of this situation. He knew that Lazarus' death was not final, and that in a matter of moments, Lazarus would walk out of the tomb alive. Yet, He did not rush past the grief of the moment. Instead, He paused to weep with those who were mourning, entering fully into their sorrow. This shows us that Jesus' love is not transactional—it is not based solely on the miracles He performs or the power He displays. His love is deeply compassionate and empathetic. He cares about the emotional and spiritual well-being of the people He loves. By weeping, Jesus demonstrated that He is not only concerned with the end result of our trials but also with the pain and suffering we experience along the way. His love meets us in our grief, walks with us through our darkest moments, and offers comfort in the midst of our sorrow.

Jesus' love for Lazarus, Mary, and Martha reflects His love for all of humanity. The tears He shed at Lazarus' tomb were not only for the loss of a friend; they were for all who experience the pain of death and loss. Jesus' love is not limited to a select few; it extends to everyone who suffers, mourns, or feels the weight of the brokenness of this world. His tears are a testament to His deep care for each one of us. They remind us that we are not alone in our suffering—Jesus is with us, feeling our pain and offering us His love and comfort. The people who witnessed Jesus' tears were moved by His obvious love for Lazarus, but they could not fully comprehend the breadth and depth of that love. Jesus' love is not just for those who were physically present with Him during His time on earth; it is a love that transcends time and space, reaching out to each one of us in our moments of need.

Moreover, Jesus' tears reveal the personal nature of His relationship with each of us. Jesus knew Lazarus, Mary, and Martha intimately. He had spent time in their home, shared meals with them, and developed a close friendship with them. His weeping shows that His love is not distant or impersonal. Jesus did not love Lazarus from afar; He was deeply involved in his life and cared about him as a person. This personal investment in the lives of those He loves is a key aspect of Jesus' character. He is not a detached or aloof deity; He is a Savior who knows us intimately, cares about every detail of our lives, and shares in our joys and sorrows. His tears at Lazarus' tomb remind us that Jesus' love is not just a general, overarching love for humanity; it is a specific, personal love for each individual. He knows our names, our struggles, our heartaches, and He weeps with us in our pain.

In addition to being a demonstration of His love for Lazarus, Mary, and Martha, Jesus' tears also reveal His love for all of humanity in the face of sin and death. Death is the ultimate consequence of sin, and it brings with it pain, separation, and grief. Jesus wept because He saw the devastation that death causes in the lives of those He loves. He was deeply moved by the sorrow and suffering that sin and death had brought into the world, and His tears reflected His desire to bring healing and restoration. Jesus' love for humanity is not just about offering eternal life; it is about entering into the pain of the human experience and bringing hope in the midst of that pain. His tears at Lazarus' tomb show that He cares deeply about the suffering that death causes, and they point to His ultimate mission to defeat death and bring life to all who believe in Him.

Furthermore, Jesus' tears reveal the compassionate nature of His love. Compassion is more than just feeling sympathy for someone's pain; it is a deep, emotional response that moves one to action. Jesus' tears were not just an emotional reaction to the grief of the moment; they were a demonstration of His compassion for those who were mourning. He was not content to simply feel their pain; He was moved to act on their behalf. By raising Lazarus from the dead, Jesus showed that His love is not passive but active. His compassion moved Him to intervene in the situation and bring life where there had been death. This is a powerful reminder that Jesus' love is not just a feeling; it is a force that brings transformation and hope. His love does not leave us in our pain; it reaches into the darkest places of our lives and brings healing, restoration, and new life.

The reaction of the people who witnessed Jesus' tears is also significant. When they saw Him weep, they said, "Behold how he loved him!" (John 11:36). This statement reveals that Jesus' love was evident to those around Him. His tears were not hidden or restrained; they were a visible sign of His deep affection for Lazarus. This public display of emotion showed the people that Jesus' love was real, personal, and genuine. It was not a distant or theoretical love; it was a love that was expressed in real, tangible ways. Jesus' weeping was a powerful testimony to the depth of His love, and it challenged those who witnessed it to reconsider their understanding of who He was. His love was not the love of a distant ruler or a detached religious figure; it was the love of a close friend who cared deeply about the people in His life.

Jesus' tears also teach us that His love is compassionate and empathetic. He does not stand apart from our suffering, observing it from a distance; He enters into it with us. His tears at Lazarus' tomb show us that Jesus is not indifferent to our pain. He feels it with us, and He weeps with us in our moments of grief. This is a profound comfort for those who are struggling with loss or heartache. Jesus' love is not just about providing solutions or fixing problems; it is about walking with us through the valleys of life, offering His presence and His comfort. His tears remind us that we are never alone in our suffering. Jesus is with us, sharing in our pain and offering us His love and compassion.

Finally, Jesus' weeping at Lazarus' tomb points to the ultimate demonstration of His love—His sacrifice on the cross. The tears He shed for Lazarus reflected the greater love that would lead Him to lay down His life for all of humanity. Jesus' love is not limited to moments of empathy or compassion; it is a sacrificial love that gives everything for the sake of those He loves. By raising Lazarus from the dead, Jesus demonstrated His power over death, but by going to the cross, He would conquer death once and for all. His tears at Lazarus' tomb foreshadow the greater sacrifice He would make to bring eternal life to all who believe in Him. Jesus' love is not just about comforting us in our grief; it is about giving us the hope of resurrection and eternal life through His death and resurrection.

In conclusion, the Demonstration of His Love at Lazarus' tomb is one of the most powerful expressions of Jesus' compassion, empathy, and personal investment in the lives of those He loves. His tears were a visible sign of His deep affection for Lazarus, Mary, and Martha, and they revealed His genuine care for their suffering. Jesus' love is not distant or impersonal; it is personal, compassionate, and real. His weeping shows us that He is fully engaged in our lives, sharing in our pain and offering us His comfort. Jesus' love is not just about performing miracles; it is about entering into our suffering and bringing hope and healing. His tears remind us that we are never alone in our grief; Jesus is with us, weeping with us and offering us His love. Ultimately, His love is a sacrificial love that gives everything to bring us eternal life, and His tears at Lazarus' tomb point to the greater sacrifice He would make on the cross for the sake of all humanity.

Conclusion

The lessons from John 11 reveal the profound depth of Jesus' compassion and His divine response to human suffering. These lessons show us that Jesus' tears at the tomb of Lazarus were not only a response to the immediate sorrow of those around Him but a reflection of His deep empathy, love, and understanding of the brokenness in the world. Through these lessons, we see that Jesus wept not just for a single moment in time but for all of humanity's pain and suffering, offering a powerful reminder that He is a Savior who cares deeply for us and is actively involved in our lives.

Jesus' tears reveal His personal investment in human suffering. Each lesson—whether it was about Death's Devastation, Doubt of the People, or Desire for Restoration—reminds us that Jesus feels the weight of our burdens and experiences our grief alongside us. His weeping demonstrates that He is not a distant God but one who enters into our pain, weeping with us and offering comfort and hope. His compassion is not superficial or fleeting; it is deep, real, and enduring. Jesus' love for Lazarus, Mary, and Martha reflects His love for all of us, reminding us that He is with us in our darkest moments, sharing in our sorrow and offering us hope in the midst of despair.

Moreover, these lessons invite us to trust in Jesus' power, love, and ultimate victory over death. Jesus' tears were not a sign of weakness but a testament to His divine purpose. His weeping was followed by the powerful act of raising Lazarus from the dead, a miracle that pointed to His own resurrection and His triumph over sin and death. This victory offers us the ultimate hope that, in Jesus, death is not the end but the beginning of new life. Through these lessons, we are called to trust in Jesus as the resurrection and the life, placing our faith in His ability to overcome the brokenness of the world and to bring us into eternal life with Him.

For Christians today, these lessons present a compelling challenge: How will we continue in our walk with Christ, trusting in His power, love, and promises, even in the face of suffering and doubt? Jesus' tears call us to reflect on how we respond to our own pain and the pain of others. Do we trust that He is with us in our suffering? Are we willing to follow His example of compassion and empathy, sharing in the burdens of others and offering them the hope that Jesus provides?

As we conclude this journey through the story of why Jesus wept, we are reminded that His tears were not just a response to the moment but a message to all of us: that He loves us, understands our pain, and desires to bring healing, restoration, and hope to a broken world. The challenge for us is to live in the light of that love, trusting in His power, and sharing that hope with others, knowing that in Jesus, even in the face of death, there is always life.

Don't miss out!

Visit the website below and you can sign up to receive emails whenever Joshua Rhoades publishes a new book. There's no charge and no obligation.

https://books2read.com/r/B-A-AJLBB-JKQAF

BOOKS2READ

Connecting independent readers to independent writers.

Did you love *Why Did Jesus Weep??* Then you should read *Restoration - Setting The Bone*[1] by Joshua Rhoades!

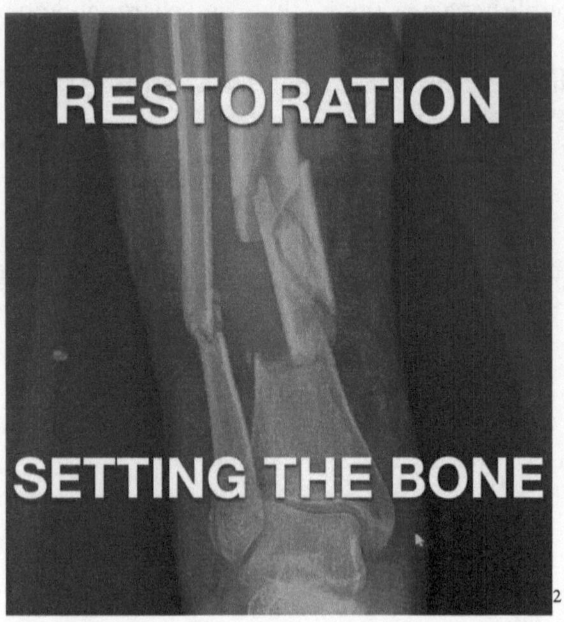

[2]

"Restoration - Setting the Bone" dives into the biblical concept of restoration, guiding Christians on their journey to wholeness after experiencing spiritual, emotional, or moral brokenness. Just as a doctor carefully sets a fractured bone to heal properly, God's restoration process involves deliberate actions to realign us with His will, mend our brokenness, and restore us to spiritual health.

The imagery of setting a bone is powerful in describing this process. A broken bone that isn't properly treated can lead to ongoing pain and dysfunction. Similarly, when spiritual fractures—caused by sin, trauma, or life's trials—are ignored, they can result in prolonged spiritual pain and hinder our ability to fulfill God's purpose. This book serves as a guide for those seeking God's loving and methodical restoration.

The Bible is filled with examples of God's restorative work. From the fall of Adam and Eve to King David's repentance after his sins, Scripture teaches that no

---

1. https://books2read.com/u/3RyQ2p

2. https://books2read.com/u/3RyQ2p

matter how broken we are, God is willing and able to restore us. In Psalm 51:10, David's plea, "Create in me a clean heart, O God; and renew a right spirit within me," encapsulates the essence of seeking restoration—recognizing our brokenness and asking God to heal and renew us.

Restoration isn't always quick or easy. Like setting a bone, it can be painful and requires time to heal. It often involves difficult steps such as confession, repentance, forgiveness, and trusting God with the future. Yet, just as a properly set bone becomes strong again, a soul restored by God emerges more resilient and better equipped to fulfill His purpose.

"Restoration: Setting the Bone" walks you through the biblical principles of restoration, offering insights into how God heals our deepest wounds and how we can cooperate with Him in this process. Whether you're seeking restoration for yourself or helping someone else, this book provides the tools and encouragement to embrace God's healing power. It reminds us that no matter how fractured our lives may seem, God is a master at setting the bone, guiding us gently and lovingly toward complete restoration.